Also by Cheryl Anderson Wright

High Country Herbs
High Altitude Growing, Gifting & Cooking with Herbs

HIGH COUNTRY
TOMATO
HANDBOOK

Including
How to Grow Ripe Tomatoes
by the 4th of July!

Cheryl Anderson Wright

www.pronghornpress.org

To all the beautiful, independent,
strong, and intelligent women
who play a part in my life;
friends who are family
and family who are friends.

Introduction

I love tomatoes. I have always loved ripe, juicy, sun-warmed tomatoes fresh from the garden more than almost anything. If someone asked me, "If you could only have one vegetable, which would you pick?" the answer would be, "Tomatoes!"

When I was a kid, my dad grew about a hundred tomato plants every year. At the first sign of a ripe tomato, I would grab the salt shaker and head for the garden. A little wipe on the shirt, a little sprinkle of salt, and I was off to my particular form of heaven.

My brother Larry hated tomatoes almost as much as I loved them. So when Mom made BLTs in the summer time for lunch, we would trade. I would give him all my lettuce and he would give me all his tomatoes. We both thought we got the best of the deal. Now Larry likes tomatoes. He has eleven kids, so I guess he learned to like anything the kids didn't eat first. But maybe he simply "grew up and got good sense" like Mom always said he would.

When you say "tomatoes" to me, I feel like Bubba in *Forest Gump.* I start right in saying, "You can eat them plain or in a salad. You can juice them, can them, freeze them, pickle them or dry them. You can make tomato soup or bread. You can stew them, bake them, boil them or fry them. You can make them into a sauce. You can serve tomatoes with every meal of the day."
I could go on and on, but you get the picture.

Here is a short poem written by Johanna M. Bolton that expresses my thoughts precisely:

I Hate Tomatoes

I hate tomatoes,
the pallid things from the grocery store,
waxy, cold, and artificially red,
their hard icy flesh with no taste at all,
and seeds that you find a week later
stuck somewhere
halfway down the front of the kitchen cabinet.
Now how did that get there?

I hate these tomatoes.

But
out in my garden, tucked here and there,
they grow, scattered among the herbs,
where the squirrels haven't found them yet,
among the bushes of rosemary and the roses,
ripening,
tiny round spheres,
one of them already glowing red
and brighter every day.
Ripening,
until I can wait no longer, and it drops,

warm and soft into my hand.
I hold it and breathe it in
for isn't scent the essence of taste?
This little tomato smells as if it was grown
in a garden beneath a canopy
of tattered green lace,
it smells of primal powers
collected in a tiny red sphere;
it smells of sun and soil,
of the four elements —
of fire, air, earth, and water ...

I hold it between my lips,
soft, round,
oh, so, smooth,
it slips between my teeth,
and I bite,
gentle pressure,
just enough to pierce the skin,
and the juice runs into my mouth.
My eyes are closed so nothing can intrude
and diminish
the incredible
sweetness
flooding the backs of my teeth,
my tongue,

palate,
throat.

And the taste,
oh, the taste!
Of fire,
of air,
earth,
and
water.

Now that's a tomato!

— *Johanna Bolton*

Contents

Cheryl Anderson Wright

When I first moved to Wyoming, I had to learn how to garden. Now, I had gardened all of my life, but in Iowa, where I was born and raised, you just planted stuff and it grew. If you spilled seeds on the way to the garden, they grew. You didn't even have to try and they grew. Not so in Wyoming. In Wyoming, you have to know what you are doing and work hard at doing it. The only things that "just grow" in Wyoming are sage, greasewood and Russian olive trees. When I moved to Wyoming in the 1970s, I lived on the South Fork of the Shoshone River, west of Cody.

The soil on our place was so bad I couldn't even grow Russian olives, let alone anything else. A kind neighbor tilled my ground for me and I had the loveliest crop of poverty weed and field bindweed you ever saw, but nothing else. The wind, frost, snow, alkali, and critters got anything that I did manage to get started, which in truth, wasn't much. I soon figured out that unless I wanted to learn how to cook those things that would "just grow" in this country, I had better learn to garden. So began my education in the world of horticulture.

I visited the county extension office and picked up every handout and brochure they had on how to improve soil, what to plant, when to plant, and the length of the growing season. I have found that some years the length of the growing season is the biggest joke this country can play on gardeners. Several times, I lost my entire garden on July 3rd or 4th. Sometimes this was the last frost of the year, quickly followed by the first one of autumn on August 1st. Many years, the last snowstorm of the year comes around the middle of June and the first snowstorm of the next year hits around the first to the middle of September. This doesn't leave a very long season, so you have to learn to do what you can to make the most of it.

For the first few years we lived here, I never harvested a single ripe tomato. Friends and family coming from Iowa would ask if they should bring anything to us on their visits. My answer was always the same: "garden-ripe tomatoes!" Whenever I went to Iowa on vacation, I would be on the lookout for tomatoes. In Wyoming, I haunted the farmers' markets and the traveling vendors in search of that red holy grail.

When all these ways and means provided too few tomatoes to satisfy my longing, I finally became desperate enough to get serious about learning how to get a ripe tomato out of this difficult country. I talked to other gardeners who told me it could be done in Powell, a town of slightly lower altitude and warmer clime just north of us, but it was nearly impossible in Cody. So I began to look for ways to extend Cody's hopelessly short season, to keep my plants warm at night and to protect them from the wind.

I discovered "walls of water," which filled the bill on all counts. Then I studied more to find the exact nutritional requirements of a tomato. I read books and books and more books. I asked the county extension agent. I asked successful gardeners and I finally came up with a method that not only guarantees that I can raise ripe tomatoes, but I can usually have my first ripe tomato by the 4th of July.

As I talked to people I found that I was not the only one who was in pursuit of the same holy grail, a vine-ripened tomato. Most people told me it was impossible in Cody, let alone up the South Fork.

And that's why I decided to write this book. I *have* learned how to grow ripe tomatoes in Cody. I *grew* them up South Fork. And I want to share that knowledge with you. It will take some effort on your part, but if you follow the instructions in this book, you *will* have ripe tomatoes.

It depends on how much effort you want to invest as to whether or not you have them by the 4th of July. And no matter where you live and garden, in a difficult climate or not, a homegrown ripe tomato is a treasure to behold *and* to consume!

A Little Tomato History

Cheryl Anderson Wright

The tomato is native to the Americas. As early as 700 C.E., both Aztecs and Incas cultivated it. In the 16th century, when the Spanish came to the New World, they found the tomato and took it back to Europe. It soon made a place for itself in Spain, and shortly thereafter in France, Italy and Portugal.

But mystery followed the tomato on its journey north from the Mediterranean countries. The French called it "The Apple of Love." The British, while admiring its brilliant red color, thought the fruit was poisonous. In northern Europe the tomato plant was associated with the poisonous members of the Solanceae family, most especially Deadly Nightshade, which it closely resembles.

Deadly nightshade, *Astopus Belladonna*, is a poisonous plant that was used as both a hallucinogenic drug and as a beauty aid in different parts of Europe. The Latin name *belladonna* literally means "beautiful woman." In medieval courts, ladies would use a few drops of nightshade extract in their eyes to make their pupils dilate, a look that was the height of fashion. This practice was continued by early film actors to keep their eyes dilated under bright lights. The hallucinogenic properties of the plant cause visions and the sense of flying. This most likely led to the association of Nightshade with witchcraft.

Old German folklore has it that witches used Nightshade to call werewolves. The common German name for tomatoes translates to "wolf peach," and so tomatoes were avoided for obvious reasons. In the 18th century, Carl Linnaeus named the tomato *Lycopersicon Esculentum*, which literally means, "edible wolf peach".

The first tomato to reach Europe was a yellow variety called "golden apple" in Italy. It was small and rough skinned, probably the same variety grown by the Aztec's near present day Mexico City. Two Catholic priests brought the first red tomato to Italy many years later.

Being mainly of British descent, colonists in the United States followed the English belief that the tomato was poisonous and so, in the beginning, most colonists grew tomatoes only as ornamentals. Some people believed tomatoes would draw infection from a wound, so they were also valued for this property. In 1781, Thomas

Jefferson brought tomatoes to his table, but few people followed suit. Later, George Washington Carver, the man who made peanut butter a household item, tried to get his poor Alabama neighbors to add tomatoes to their woefully vitamin deficient diet, but met with only limited success. Early merchants could not get people to even taste the fruit.

The Louisiana Purchase added a great amount of land to the U.S. and by 1812, the Creoles in New Orleans were enhancing the flavor of their gumbos and jambalayas with the addition of tomatoes. At the opposite end of the country, the people of Maine quickly followed suit, combining fresh tomatoes with local seafood.

Although New Orleans had adopted the tomato, many northerners remained highly suspicious of the safety of eating them. In 1820, a farm journal reported that Colonel Robert Gibbon Johnson, at noon on September 26th, would eat a bushel of tomatoes in front of the Boston courthouse. The story goes that thousands of eager spectators turned out to watch the poor man die and were shocked when he survived the ordeal. While this story may be more entertaining than truthful, tomatoes began to steadily grow in popularity thereafter.

Soon, cookbooks began including recipes calling for tomatoes. By 1835, tomatoes were found for sale in markets in Boston and in 1847, Thomas Bridgeman listed four varieties of seed in his catalogue. The tomato then gained a huge following in a relatively short period of time. In 1858, a seed merchant named Buist commented: "In taking retrospect of the last eighteen years, there is no vegetable in the catalogue that has obtained such popularity in so short a period as the one now under consideration. In 1828-29, it was almost detested; in ten years most every variety of pill and panacea was extract of tomato. It now occupies as great a surface of ground as cabbage, and is cultivated the length and breadth of the country."

By 1850, the tomato was accepted all over the United States. People were planting tomatoes in their home gardens and farmers in warmer areas began commercial production

By 1863, one seed catalogue listed twenty-three varieties, among which was Trophy, the first modern-looking large, red, smooth-skinned variety, which fetched the princely sum of five dollars for a packet of twenty seeds. By the late 1800s, it was clear that the tomato had firmly implanted itself in western culture.

The argument about the tomato as fruit or vegetable may be older than you imagine. In 1883, the U.S. passed a tariff act requiring a 10% tax on imported vegetables. A few years later an importer decided to challenge the law, in part on the grounds that a tomato was, in fact, technically a fruit, not a vegetable and should therefore be exempt from said tax. In 1893, John Nix's case landed before the Supreme Court. In Nix vs. Hedden, Justice Gray wrote: *Botanically speaking, tomatoes are fruits of a vine, just as are cucumbers, squashes, beans, and peas. But in the common language of the people...all these are vegetables, which are grown in kitchen gardens, and which, whether eaten cooked or raw, are, like potatoes, carrots, parsnips, turnips, beets, cauliflower, cabbage, celery and lettuce, usually served at dinner in, with or after the soup, fish or meats which constitute the principal part of the repast, and not, like fruits generally, as dessert.* The Supreme Court ruled the tomato a vegetable and so it remains to this day.

Now we have many named varieties or cultivars, somewhere over 171. There are hybrids, open pollinated and heirloom selections. Tomatoes come in many colors and shapes. Some are black, dark purple, green, white, orange or yellow. Some are one solid color and others have green stripes. Some are rainbow colored, some are pear shaped and some are hollow. There are cherry size varieties while others weigh in at over two pounds.

Many heirloom varieties have colorful histories as well. A West Virginian named Charlie, who owned a radiator repair shop that fell on hard times during the Great Depression, bred a tomato he named "the Mortgage Lifter." He used the four largest-fruited tomato plants he had and crossed them repeatedly with each other to create a plant that produced two-pound fruits. He sold the plants for a dollar each, claiming one plant would feed a family of six. Within four years, he had made enough money to pay off the four thousand dollar mortgage on his house!

Names of heirloom cultivars often reflect some of the history of the plant. *Amish Paste* is a variety that has been grown by the Amish in Pennsylvania since the 1870s. Amish farmers near Brandywine Creek in Chester County, Pennsylvania developed *Brandywine* in 1885. *Hillbilly* came from the hills of West Virginia.

Heirloom tomatoes breed true to their parents, so you can save your own seed to grow next year's crop. Heirlooms definitely present greater diversity, but typically have lower yields and lower disease resistance.

The seed from hybrids, on the other hand, may take on the characteristics of either of the parents, or even the grandparents or they may be sterile. This is the very property that makes hybrids so attractive to seed producers since it ensures that customers must buy new seed each year. Many people argue that hybrids are bred for size and yield rather than taste, while the heirloom has always placed flavor first. Hybrid varieties have historically looked and tasted very similar to each other.

Tomatoes have even found a place in Hollywood history. The late sixties sci-fi flick *Attack of the Killer Tomatoes* entertained millions, but scared no one — unlike the 1981 ruling by the USDA chairman who declared ketchup to be considered as a serving of a vegetable in order to justify Reagan administration budget cuts in the school lunch program. That ruling should scare *everyone* as the only nutritious part of ketchup is the tomato.

The most recent contribution to tomato breeding has been biotechnology. For years merchants have tried to find a good tasting product which ships well. Because ripe tomatoes have a very short shelf life and bruise easily, growers pick the tomatoes green and ship them to other locations, often thousands of miles away. The green fruits are firm and resist bruising. They are usually red by the time they reach their destination, or they can be induced to ripen with the application of an ethylene spray. But consumers complain about the lack of flavor.

In the 1980s a project was undertaken by Calgene Fresh, Inc. using biotechnology to inactivate the gene responsible for softening the tomato during ripening. These tomatoes turned red, but remained firm indefinitely. They could be vine ripened, giving the tomato a great flavor, and still be firm enough to be shipped. They called this cultivar Flavr Savr. It hit the produce sections of stores in the U.S. during 1993. The Flavr Savr tomato represents one of the greatest public relations blunders of the decade. Industry failed to recognize the public's fear of genetically engineered food. Although evidence suggesting any danger in genetically engineered food is lacking, consumers remain nervous about potentially unknown and unforeseen side effects. The Flavr Savr tomato was removed from supermarket shelves, and has never been reintroduced.

The latest news surrounding tomatoes is the reported benefit of lycopene, the major carotenoid contained in tomatoes. It is the ingredient responsible for the deep red color. Similar to beta-carotene, lycopene has been touted as a potent anti-oxidant, a molecule that rids the body of cancer-causing free radicals. Results from cancer research have already driven tomato breeders at the University of Florida to produce high lycopene cultivars such as the currant tomato, which produces tiny fruits containing over forty times more lycopene than regular tomatoes.

And so today we find the top five tomato producing countries of the world are the United States, China, Turkey, Italy and India, in that order. An estimated thirty-five million backyard gardens across the country grow tomatoes. Tomatoes rank high as a source for vitamins A and C. They also contain significant amounts of lycopene, beta-carotene, magnesium, niacin, iron, phosphorus, potassium, riboflavin, sodium and thiamine. A University of California at Davis survey ranked the tomato as the single most important fruit or vegetable of western diets in terms of an overall source of vitamins and minerals.

After only a few hundred years, the tomato has firmly implanted itself as a major player in diets of many nationalities. Italian cooking has become synonymous with tomato sauce. Where would pizza or spaghetti be without it? Where would Mexican restaurants be without salsa? Tomato soup, slices on a burger and ketchup are all highly integrated uses for the versatile vegetable in American culture. Additionally, millions of Americans grow tomatoes in their backyards each year. From one continent to another, the tomato has made an important place for itself in cultures around the globe.

Cheryl Anderson Wright

Soils

Cheryl Anderson Wright

If you intend to grow anything, tomatoes included, the place to start is with your soil. Remember, you have to "feed" the soil if you want your soil to grow the plants to feed you.

The way to find out how good your soil is or what it needs is through a soil test. You can go to the county extension office and get a soil test kit. It will come with complete instructions for exactly how to proceed and where to send it once you have your sample ready to go. And when you get the test results back you'll know your soil pH, fertility level, how much organic matter it contains, and what you need to add. If you don't know what to do with the results, your extension agent will be glad to help you. This test will cost about twenty dollars, but it is money well spent. You are probably going to get sick of me telling you this, but this soil test is the most important thing you can do for your garden.

There are five standard requirements for any garden:

- Healthy soil filled with organic matter and living organisms
- Heat
- Water
- Sunlight
- A near neutral pH

You can do things to enhance the temperature in your garden. Your climate and area of the country will dictate the number of hours of sunlight you receive and the initial pH of your soil. But you can add amendments to change the soil pH. You can locate your garden to receive the maximum amount of sunlight. You can make sure your plants have the amount of water they need. You can add row covers or use mulch or walls of water to make the environment warmer. However, I cannot emphasize soil condition enough, regardless of where you are gardening. If you do not have a fertile, fast draining soil filled with organic matter, your chances of growing much more than weeds is nil.

Soil is made up of clay, sand and loam. Soil in the Rocky Mountain west is usually clay or sand. Clay soils are made up of tiny particles that cling closely together when wet. Clay soils will hold this water and drown any plants unlucky enough to be planted in it. You will need to add all the organic matter you can get to get a good arable soil.

In some parts of the Rockies you will find soil that consists mainly of sand. Sandy soils are composed of such large particles they will not bond together. Thus, sandy soils will not retain enough water to support plant life. Once again you will need to add organic matter to it to get it into condition for growing plants.

And loam is that wonderful black rich soil that you find in the Midwest; the kind of soil you find in the bags labeled "Top Soil". If you amend your soil enough you can produce a rich clay/loam soil but it will take several years to accomplish.

Soil pH is simply a measure of the acidity or alkalinity of the soil, with 7 being neutral, 7 to 14 being alkaline and 7 to 0 being acidic. Soil pH determines the availability of nutrients to the plants. For example, in the alkaline soils of the Rocky Mountains, the soil usually contains plenty of iron, but that iron is chemically tied up so is unavailable to plants, which means you might need to spray an iron foliate on your plants.

You will probably need to add amendments to the soil to bring it to a more neutral pH, as most plants prefer a soil that is slightly acidic, in the range of 5.0 to 6.8, though many plants will tolerate a pH as high as 7.6, which is closer to the pH of amended soil here in the mountains.

0	7	14
Acid	Neutral	Alkaline

Sulfur will lower your pH, as will gypsum. Gypsum will not only lower the pH, but will also add calcium. Coffee grounds are acidic and high in nitrogen.

You may also need to add nutrients. Our soils are notorious for lacking in nitrogen. Most manures and blood meal will add nitrogen, as will grass clippings. Kelp meal will add over sixty trace elements to your soil. Eggshells are high in calcium. Homemade compost will add nitrogen, phosphorous and potassium as well as other trace elements depending on what you add to it. Peat moss adds organic matter and lowers the pH. Well-rotted sawdust also adds organic matter. Leaves make great additions to your soil. All your kitchen scraps – vegetable peelings, outside leaves of lettuce and cabbage, tea bags, coffee grounds, tough stems of asparagus – all make great additions to your garden. And besides, look how much garbage you will save from the landfill if you simply till it into your garden. Everybody wins.

Wood ashes are one thing you do **not** want to add to your garden or your compost. They are alkaline and will raise your already too high pH even higher.

Cheryl Anderson Wright

Composting

Cheryl Anderson Wright

Now I need to put in a few words about composting. Most people who garden will sooner or later try their hand at it. Composting can take many forms. You can buy a kitchen composter and simply follow the formula to compost your kitchen scraps. This is a good option if you live in an apartment and would still like to try your hand at composting. Regardless of your living and garden situation, these items can all be a part of your compost.

Compost Ingredients:

- Coffee grounds and tea leaves
- Eggshells
- Trimmings from bushes and trees,
  (especially if you have a chipper/shredder)

- Kitchen waste from vegetables, fruits and grains
- Lawn clippings
- Pine needles
- Leaves
- Shredded paper or newspaper
- Old straw or hay
- Weeds and disease-free plant debris
- Aged sawdust or wood shavings
- Blood meal, bonemeal, kelp meal
- Manure (from an herbivore, aged if possible)

Never use diseased plant debris, or plants that have had pesticides or herbicides used on them.

Never use meat, bones, grease or cooking oils.

Never use cat or dog manure, as these may contain parasites that could be transferred to humans.

The materials you do use should be in the smallest pieces you can manage. If you don't have a chipper/shredder you can lay materials down in thin layers and run over them with your lawn mower, then rake them up and put them in the compost pile.

There are many different composting containers or systems available on the market. You can buy one of these if you are so inclined. If you don't want to spend the money (most of these devices are expensive) you can simply pile your organic matter in the yard, somewhere out of the sight of your neighbors, but preferably near your garden.

You can enclose it in a simple piece of woven wire fencing. You build an H shape from the palettes that many lumberyards and hardware stores are willing to give away. You can layer one side and then throw it to the other side, instead of simply turning your pile. If you are going to turn your compost pile, it is a good idea to do it about once a week.

If you are lazy, like I am, or simply pressed for time, you can buy a heavy black plastic garbage can, drill some holes in the bottom and sides and set it up on some bricks or pieces of 4x4. Put three or four inches of soil or compost in the bottom of it and then start filling it as instructed below. Keep the lid on it between additions. You usually don't even have to add any water to this kind of composter.

The main thing in composting in my arid country is getting the right mix and right moisture content to start the pile turning into something you can use in your garden. Finding this essential mix is the all-important key to successful composting.

The usual formula is two to three inches of green material (this might be kitchen scraps or grass clippings) to two inches of dry material (sawdust, manure, leaves, old hay or straw). And throwing in a scoop or two of soil here and there is helpful to get things going.

Very few people I know have the right amounts of organics available to be quite so scientific about it. What

Cheryl Anderson Wright

I do is this: after I dump three or four small buckets of kitchen scraps on my pile, I add a couple of inches of old leaves or some shredded paper from my office. Then a scoop or two of manure, then more kitchen scraps, more leaves or paper and more manure. (I use composted manure that I buy. It has no weed seeds, I don't have to go to a farm and scoop it, and it doesn't smell!)

When my bin is full, I water it and add a good layer of soil. Then I cover it with a piece of landscape fabric and let it sit until it composts. And, the truth is, despite whether you have all the proportions right or not, any pile of organic stuff will turn to compost if it sits long enough.

The exception to all the steps above comes in the spring when I am raking leaves. I rake a big pile of leaves into a black plastic bag, add two or three scoops of manure, dump in a bucket of water, put a twisty tie on the bag and put it in a sunny corner until fall; easy compost that is ready to use to put the garden to bed.

Cheryl Anderson Wright

Pests

Cheryl Anderson Wright

We don't have as many pests here in the high desert country of the Rockies as they have in the fertile East. That is the good news. The bad news is the ones we do have are tough and persistent, just like everything else in this country. Even so, I only use organic pesticides and so that is all I will talk about here. If you want to use chemicals, and that is a choice you will have to make, then by all means do so. I personally think we have enough pollutants in our food and environment without adding more.

I also like to use row covers on the cabbage family of plants. Row covers extend your season a little bit by keeping the frost off the leaves, and they keep egg laying moths off your plants. They can be purchased from nurseries or nursery catalogues.

Aphids: If you look at the underside of the leaves of your plants and see bunches of very small black, pink, green, gray, or white bugs they are probably aphids. If you also see a sticky substance on the leaves you can be almost certain you have an aphid infestation. If you see ants all over the plant this is another sign of aphids. The ants are there to "milk" the aphids for that sticky stuff, which is called honeydew.

If you only have a few leaves infested, try picking off the leaves and disposing of them. If there are too many to pick off, try knocking the aphids off with frequent strong sprays of water from the hose. If water doesn't work, try washing or spraying the plant with an insecticidal soap. As a last resort, you can spray with pyrethrum or rotenone or some other organic pesticide, but know that using any pesticide will also kill the beneficial insects, such as lady beetles or lacewings. I have read that putting aluminum foil over the soil of potted plants in the greenhouse will keep aphids away. I have never used this method so I am not sure it will work.

Aphids have an unusual life cycle. Aphid eggs can overwinter on woody stems and hatch in spring into "stem females," which give continuous birth to live nymphs without ever having to mate. Nymphs mature into adults in one to two weeks. These adults also bear live young. Then in the fall, males and normal females are born; these mate to produce the eggs, which overwinter. In greenhouses, where it might be warm all year, this egg producing phase may never occur.

You might want to spray fruit trees with dormant oil to attempt to kill these overwintering eggs. But be sure to follow the directions on the package or talk to your extension agent because improper use may cause more damage to your trees than the aphids will.

Colorado Potato Beetle: You might find these on any nightshade plant, such as tomato, eggplant or peppers. Most often you will see them first on the potato plants. The eggs are bright yellow ovals found on the underside of the leaves. The larvae are dark orange, humpbacked grubs with black spots along the sides. The adults are about 1/3 inch long, yellowish orange beetles with black stripes on their backs.

If you don't have too many beetles you can pick them off by hand. When I was a kid, we all earned pocket money picking off potato bugs and eggs. Carry a bucket of soapy water or gasoline and drop the eggs, larva or beetles into it. You can try sprinkling the plants with diatomaceous earth made up of the fossilized silica shells of algae called diatoms. If necessary you can spray weekly with pyrethrin or rotenone or BT. These pests overwinter in the soil so be sure you are practicing crop rotation. Also, fall tillage of your garden space may bring the pests to the surface where birds will eat them or they will freeze.

Cutworms: I have never had a problem with cutworms here. But if you start finding new seedlings cut off right at ground level, cutworms are probably at work. Putting a stick into the ground beside the plant will usually stop the damage, as a cutworm has to be able to completely encircle the plant to cut it. Anything that will stop the cutworm from encircling the plant may be used. You can use the cardboard roll from paper towels or toilet tissue. Cut the rolls into two to three inch pieces and push them part way into the ground around your tender new seedlings. They will hold up until the plants are big enough to survive on their own. Or you can make a collar of aluminum foil, which you can remove when the plant is big enough.

Earwigs: Earwigs are not generally a problem in a garden, though they will eat lettuce and other soft vegetation. They also hide in foliage, so when you pick your lettuce and take it in to wash, you could end up with earwigs floating in your wash water. If you are squeamish this can be disconcerting, to say the least. If earwigs are a problem for you or your garden, you can lay out the cardboard tubes from paper towels and in the morning dump the earwigs out of them into a bucket of water and dispose of them. Diatomaceous earth scattered around the edges of your garden will discourage them, too. Before you decide to get rid of the earwigs in your garden remember they are predators of aphids and other small garden pests.

Grasshoppers:

In the twenty-five years I have gardened in the West, I only had trouble with grasshoppers once. They invaded in hoards and ate everything in their path right to the ground, even the marigolds, nasturtiums and petunias I had planted to repel insects. I know people who never have problems with grasshoppers and others who consider them a major pest. If they would happen to be a problem for you, I suggest that you use a product called Semaspore, which is fairly easy to find from an organic supplier. You can purchase it from Planet Natural and many other places that sell organic products.

Mealy Bugs:

These pests are much more prevalent on houseplants or in your greenhouse than on garden plants in our area. They are minute little pink things covered with a white waxy fluff. They are a sucking insect and, like aphids, excrete honeydew. Eggs are laid in a fluffy white mass on the plant. You can wash the mealy bugs off, being meticulous and sure to get every one. You can spray with insecticidal soap. If your plant has deep folds or is heavily infested, cut your loses and throw it away before other plants get infected.

Slugs: Slugs are those gross "snails without shells" that leave trails of slime in their wake and desimate your whole row of lettuce in one night. If you have raised beds, you can put a copper flashing around the edges of the beds. You can trap slugs under boards or flowerpots and dump them into a bucket of salt water. You can shake salt on them. You can bury shallow pans of beer in the garden so the lip of the pan is at the same level as the soil. You can put crushed eggshells around your plants or you can use diatomaceous earth. Diatomaceous earth is the fossilized silica shells of algae called diatoms. The microscopic shells are very sharp and cut the body of the slug, causing them to die. If you choose to use this, place the diatomaceous earth in an old saltshaker and sprinkle it on and around the plants you wish to protect. Wear a mask when you sprinkle this or any other powdery substance to avoid inhaling it. Eggshells and diatomaceous earth must be reapplied frequently, especially after each overhead watering.

When I built my first raised beds, they quickly became overrun with slugs. They were eating things faster than I could plant them. I was very busy that summer, so when someone gave me a sage plant I stuck it in the garden until I could prepare a proper herb bed. And one day I woke up and realized that I had not seen a slug in a couple of weeks. I left that sage plant there for two or three years before moving it to the herb bed. I never had another slug. I still have some herbs coming up as volunteers in my garden: borage, thyme, mint, and horseradish to name a few. Now whether the herbs deterred the slugs, I couldn't say for sure. I only know I no longer have slugs.

Spider Mites:
The creatures are so small you have to look for them through a microscope. If you don't have a microscope you can try a magnifying glass or take some leaves from the plant you suspect is infected to your county extension agent. This is another one of the sucking insects so the leaves will look pale and may drop early. They might feel dusty or grainy when you run your fingers over them. Eggs and adults will both overwinter in bark or garden debris and emerge in early spring. If your fruit trees are infested, spray them with dormant oil to kill the eggs. If you have mites in your greenhouse or garden, spray them off and mist the plants daily. If need be, you can spray with insecticidal soap, pyrethrin, or rotenone. Spider mites are generally a bigger problem in years of drought. You will more often find them on bushes and trees than in your garden.

Thrips:
If you see discolored leaves and stems and don't see any honeydew, thrips are probably your problem. These are another variety of sucking insect. Like spider mites, they are too small to see without a magnifying glass. They are more prevalent in greenhouses than in gardens.

Adults overwinter in plant debris and bark, so if you have thrips, spray with dormant oil. You can hang sticky tape in your greenhouse to catch the adults. Spraying with insecticidal soap or pyrethrum may help.

Tomato Hornworm: The caterpillar of this pest is large, about 4 1/2 inches long and green, with a black horn on the tail end and white markings along the sides. Folklore states that planting basil with tomatoes helps repel hornworm. Calendulas may help also. Many times the moth of the hornworm will lay its eggs on a Virginia Creeper, so it might be a good idea not to have any of this plant near the spot where you are trying to grow tomatoes. Hand picking the caterpillars from your plants and disposing of them is usually all the control you need, but if necessary you can spray with BT.

White Flies: Once again, this sucking insect is usually much more of a problem in the greenhouse than in the garden. The adults are minute white flying insects that fly off plants in hordes when disturbed. They lay thousands of eggs on the underside of leaves and both nymphs and adults suck juices from the plants.

They also secrete honeydew.

The eggs hatch in two days into mobile scales and

in a few days molt to a legless stage, and then go through several nymph stages. This whole process takes twenty to thirty days.

You can: hang up sticky traps, vacuum the critters off the plants, try to attract parasitic wasps and other beneficial insects, or spray with pyrethrum.

I have tried all of these things and have not found any of them to be very effective control. I finally set my plants outside. I didn't see any new white flies. Then we had a frost warning and I put the plants back into the greenhouse and the white flies renewed their attack. I closed the greenhouse with no plants in it. The temperature soared to over 120 degrees. The white flies simply basked in the warmth. The cold will kill them, but always expect a new crop next year.

Cheryl Anderson Wright

Beneficial Insects

Cheryl Anderson Wright

It is important that you learn to identify insects if you are going to manage any kind of control. For example, there are many beneficial insects; insects that eat the pests that eat your crops. An overall insecticide is going to kill these beneficial insects as well as the pests, so know what you are killing before you just indiscriminately start applying a pesticide. Ladybugs, praying mantis, lace wings, earwigs, yellow jackets, tachinid flies, soldier bugs, parasitic nematodes, honey bees, hover flies, ground beetles, centipedes, bumble bees, bigeyed bugs, assassin bugs, aphid midges and pirate bugs are some of the many beneficial insects you want to encourage in your garden.

You can buy the egg cases for some of these insects from places like Gardens Alive. Some, like ladybugs, are shipped live. You can also plant the things these predators like such as flowering plants and herbs to attract them to your garden. Rock or stone paths in the garden will also give beneficial insects a place to find shelter.

Cheryl Anderson Wright

Plant Diseases

Cheryl Anderson Wright

Many of the things that cause problems with plants in this part of the country find their beginnings in our poor soils. Soil with a high pH for example, may have plenty of iron in it, but that iron is not available to the plant because of the high pH. When the leaves of a plant turn yellow but the veins stay bright green, this is an indication of iron deficiency. A plant that produces all leaves and no fruit has too much nitrogen.

Wilt: There are several types of wilt. The most common is Verticillium Wilt, but Bacterial Wilt and Fusarium Wilt could also be present. All three cause similar symptoms: yellowing of leaves and wilting of the entire plant. The plant looks like it has not been watered or has been over-watered.

The best control for this disease is to plant resistant varieties. The variety name will be followed by certain letters to tell you which diseases the plant is resistant to:

- V = Verticillium Wilt

- F = Fusarium Wilt, with FF meaning Fusarium races 1 & 2,

- FFF = Fusarium, Races 1,2, & 3

- N = Nematodes

- T = Tobacco Mosaic Virus

- A = Alternaria Stem Canker

- St = Stemphylium Gray Leaf Spot.

Wilt can affect many plants but tomatoes are particularly susceptible.

You may want to solarize your soil. This may or may not be effective against wilt. To do this, wet the soil, and then spread a sheet of clear plastic tightly over the soil surface. Put rocks, bricks or boards along the edges to hold the plastic in place. Leave it down for several weeks. The buildup of heat will kill most soil borne pathogens and weed seeds.

Crop rotation may slow the development of wilt, but rotation alone will not stop this fungal disease.

Blossom End Rot: This disease is most commonly caused by lack of calcium. If the blossom or bottom end of your tomato gets a large brown leathery spot that appears flattened or sunken, this is blossom end rot. This is particularly easy to cure or prevent. When you plant the tomato seedling in the spring, work about a cup of bonemeal into the planting hole. Then keep the plants evenly moist with regular watering and spread down a good organic mulch.

Damping Off: This is another fungal disease that strikes seedlings. The fungi rot the stem right at the soil line and overnight, the seedling falls over. You can sprinkle a thin layer of perlite on the soil surface to keep the plants dry at the soil line; or use a layer of sphagnum moss, which will reduce the chance of fungal growth. Provide good drainage and avoid over crowding your seedlings and the problem can usually be avoided, which is always the best option.

Others Problems: Many of the other problems we see in our area are caused by our erratic, unpredictable weather. It is a country where it can be fifty degrees in the morning and ten or lower by afternoon; where you can have a ninety degree day followed by a snowstorm; where you have no rain for three months and a monsoon that drops six inches of rain in an hour.

Plants have to be tough, to say the least, to survive. As a gardener you need to have a supply of old blankets to cover plants in case of a late frost or snow. Plan your garden so the winds will have the least effect possible, even if you have to plant a windbreak or build a fence.

Animal damage is also a concern. A sweet little Bambi or Thumper is not nearly so adorable when it has just eaten your whole row of lettuce, three pots of basil and your first ripe tomato. There are all kinds of sprays and powders and other repellents available on the market. But the fact remains; the best deterrent is a tight fence, high enough so the deer can't jump it, with a small enough mesh that rabbits can't get through. And if rabbits are a problem, remember to bury the bottom of the fence in the soil so they can't dig under.

I have heard that planting garlic and onions all around the edges of your garden will keep predators out. I contend that the effectiveness of such plants as deterrents depends on how hungry the predator is and how fond it may be of garden produce. If an animal is hungry it will eat almost anything and some have a preference for a particular vegetable or fruit, just as you do.

Save yourself the frustration and fence your garden.

Cheryl Anderson Wright

Starting Your Own Plants
From Seeds

Cheryl Anderson Wright

You will need to start thinking about tomatoes in January or February if you want to have ripe tomatoes by the 4th of July. Whenever those seed catalogues start filling your mailbox, you'll know it is time to start the search for the perfect tomato.

You will want to order or buy a tomato seed that will grow well in a pot if you are going to do container gardening. *Totally Tomatoes* offers Patio Hybrid, Husky Red, and Totem Hybrid. *Seeds of Change* carries Silvery Fir Tree and Red House Free Standing. *Jung's* suggests Tumbler Hybrid and Window Box Roma Hybrid.

Although these are specifically bred for container growing, almost any tomato can be grown in a pot if that pot is large enough. If you want to try a Big Boy or a Brandywine in a container, you will want to use a half-barrel or something of that approximate size, as they grow tall, need lots of room and will need support to do well.

After you have the seeds and you know what kind of container you are going to plant the tomato in, you need to get the seeds started.

The last frost-free date in Cody is supposed to be about May 17th, though most years it snows in mid-June. But let's say, just for the sake of argument, that the date of the last frost really is May 17th. That will be the earliest you can plant outside. Before that date you will be carrying containers in and out. Count back about eight weeks to mid-March. This is the latest you will want to plant your seeds. I generally get a spell of spring fever or gardening lust around the middle of February and start my seeds then. Consider, too, that I do have a greenhouse. If you don't have a greenhouse or a really sunny south window in your house, you will probably want to wait until mid-March to plant as seedlings held too long in the house become leggy and have a difficult time adjusting to the outdoors.

I like the flats with the clear plastic covers for starting my seeds. They are like a mini greenhouse and control heat and moisture very well. I use a good seed starting mix, preferably soil-less, so that I can prevent damping off disease from ruining my good intentions. *Jiffy Mix* and *Miracle Gro* are two varieties I have used.

Most greenhouses and nurseries will carry a good type of seedling starter. Fill each cell level with this mix, firm the mix into cell lightly, then water the flat at least three times to get the mix to absorb the water necessary. When the growing medium is evenly damp, take a pencil or pointed stick and, make a small hole about 1/4 inch deep in the center of each cell. Drop one or two seeds into each little hole and water well once more. Be sure to mark each cell or row of cells with the name of the variety you have planted, unless you are only planting one kind of seed.

You may use peat pots or peat pellets, small plastic pots or even washed plastic cartons as your seeding containers. If you do use plastic containers, be sure to punch a drain hole or two in the bottom. Fill your chosen container with the soil-less mix (unless using the peat pellets) and tamp down lightly. Water the soil well and allow the containers to sit until the water is absorbed and the container has drained well. You can drop the peat pellets into the trays made for them or into clean yogurt containers and add water until they swell and won't absorb any more water. Now you are ready to plant the same way as directed above. Cover each container with plastic wrap held on with a rubber band and place the pots in a warm spot, in a leak proof tray.

At this point you do not need light, but you do need heat to get the seeds to germinate, which will take seven to fourteen days at a temperature of seventy to eighty degrees. You can set the trays on top of a frost-free

Cheryl Anderson Wright

refrigerator or a hot water heater if you keep your house on the cool side. Or you can get fancy like I did and buy a seedling mat, which is made for the purpose.

Once the seeds have sprouted, move the plants to the sunniest windowsill that you have. Or set the seedlings four to eight inches below grow lights for twelve to eighteen hours a day. But be sure to turn the lights off at night. Keep the plants carefully watered and provide for air circulation to prevent mold or other fungus diseases from starting. Fertilize your plants with half doses of a water-soluble fertilizer when they reach three to four weeks of age. You can transplant the seedlings when they get their first true leaf, but I like to wait until the plants are five to six inches tall.

Cheryl Anderson Wright

Greenhouses & Cold Frames

Cheryl Anderson Wright

Two other ways to raise seedlings are in a greenhouse or a cold frame. Greenhouses come in many shapes and sizes; they can be purchased or homemade. There are many good books on greenhouses and before you buy or build one, it would be a good idea to study up on the whole procedure.

I have a greenhouse that my husband built for me. It has extended my season to the point that I am now gardening about nine months out of the year in most years. And I am still learning about using it.

An easier, cheaper way to grow seedlings is in a cold frame. A cold frame is a box with a glass or plastic lid that is set on bare ground. The back of the cold frame is higher than the front and in our area, it is generally tipped toward the south to get the most benefit from the sun.

Cold frames can also be either built or purchased. Many people I know go to garage sales and buy the old wooden framed storm windows to use for the top or lid of the cold frame and then build the box according to those dimensions.

Back in Iowa, my dad had a cold frame that was about three feet wide and four feet long and he raised all the seedlings we needed for our quarter acre garden. There are many designs available in magazines and books for both greenhouses and cold frames. Many manufacturers also offer a variety of sizes and prices in both. It depends on how much money you want to spend and how much effort you want to put out as to what you get.

I know a man who is plagued by deer eating his tomatoes so he built a cold frame that measures about three feet square and four feet high. His tomatoes grow in these cold frames all year. He keeps them open in the daytime and closes them at night. He has about a dozen of them to house his tomatoes. The sides and top are green fiberglass fastened to a wooden frame. So, you see, it depends on how fond you are of early ripe tomatoes as to the lengths you are willing to go to have them!

Cheryl Anderson Wright

Buying Plants

Cheryl Anderson Wright

If this is your first time growing anything, or if you have no place to grow seedlings, or if you simply find the whole process too daunting, then buy your tomato plants.

Husky Red and Patio are the two common tomatoes you will find in most greenhouses. Some nurseries may have other cultivars suited to your purpose as well. Decide how you are going to grow your tomatoes — in pots, in raised beds, or in the ground in walls of water, and buy the most appropriate plant for you.

As I said, most tomatoes can be raised in containers if the container is big enough. If you are growing tomatoes in raised beds or in a conventional garden, then the sky's the limit. Try an old standby like Early Girl or an heirloom like Brandywine. If this is your first time growing tomatoes, you might want to stick to the hybrids, as they are somewhat easier to grow, more disease resistant and produce more tomatoes per plant.

For your first tomato you will probably want to choose a short season variety, even though many of the early varieties are also quite small.

But despite that, I like to hedge my bets and plant at least a few early varieties. I have seen it snow every month of the year since I have lived in Cody. I have seen years when we have nearly ninety frost-free (and snow free) days. I have also seen years when we have had only about thirty.

Cheryl Anderson Wright

Ripe Tomatoes
by the
4th of July

Cheryl Anderson Wright

If you intend to have ripe tomatoes by the 4th of July the transplant date is the all-important number you are looking for. It is the transplant date that determines when you will pick your first ripe tomato, not the date you plant your seeds. If you choose a Husky Red at 68 days or a Patio at 70 days, then count back from the 4th of July that many days. You are going to have to have that tomato transplanted to its growing container by the April 24th or 26th respectively, if you really want ripe tomatoes by the 4th of July.

The size of the tomato plant is not important. I have purchased really large plants with blossoms and tomatoes set on and planted them next to tomato plants from a four pack. It is hard to believe, but they both had ripe tomatoes within two days of each other. This proves that it is not the size of the plant that matters. You will want to choose nice healthy, sturdy plants. That is much more important than size.

Here in the Rockies, in our harsh climate, I do have ripe tomatoes by the first part of July more years than not. For you, it will depend on how important it is to accomplish this and how much effort you are willing to expend.

I want to have all the garden ripe tomatoes I can get over the longest season possible, so this is very important to me. And most years I accomplish it, though it is much easier since I've had a greenhouse. But I still had ripe tomatoes by the 4th of July for many years before I acquired it.

Hardening Off

"Hardening off" is a term you will want to become familiar with if you are going to be successful. On that first warm day of late spring, you put on your shorts and tank top and run to the garden or the lake, and because it is so warm and the sun is shining so brightly and you are so sick of dreary winter, you stay all day. And what happens? You get sunburned and possibly wind burned because you are not used to the sun and wind.

The same thing will happen to your tender little seedlings if you stick them right out into the garden.

You will want to harden your plants before putting them outside in full sun and wind. To do this properly, set the plants out on a warm day in the shade in a sheltered area. Then next day, put them somewhere sheltered but where they will get an hour or so of direct sunlight. Move them slowly into more and more sunlight. Do this for a week before leaving them in full sun. You will want to follow this same procedure even if you buy your plants.

Cheryl Anderson Wright

Tomato Facts & Varieties

Cheryl Anderson Wright

Tomatoes are either described as "determinate" or "indeterminate". Determinate varieties stop growing at a certain stage and set all their fruit at once. They may not require staking. Indeterminate varieties grow and set fruit all season and usually require a cage or staking.

Tomatoes are also hybrid, heirloom and open pollinated. Tomatoes are self pollinating, but hybrids are deliberately cross-pollinated and bred from two or more parents to have specific traits, such as disease resistance. You can't save seed from hybrids. They won't be the same as the parent plant and in some cases the seeds are sterile.

Heirlooms are old tried and true varieties that have stood the test of time. Many people think heirlooms have better flavor than hybrids. I am one of those people. I really like heirloom tomatoes. I like experimenting with many different varieties.

Open pollinated tomatoes are those that are pollinated by wind or insects. All heirlooms are open pollinated but not all open pollinated tomatoes are heirlooms. There is a new marketing ploy afoot which labels some genetically modified varities as "open pollinated" so be aware of what you are buying. You can save your own seed from heirlooms or open pollinated tomatoes, as they will breed true to the parent plant, genetically modified or not.

Tomatoes come in many colors, sizes and shapes. Some are round, others are oblate; some are smooth, others are pleated or lobed or pear-shaped. Ripe tomatoes come in red, yellow, white, black, brown, green, orange and pink. Some are of mixed colors like Rainbow or Mr. Stripey. Some tomatoes are huge, weighing more than a pound. Others are as tiny as grapes. And tomatoes also come in every size in between. So grow the varieties that appeal to your tastes.

Here are a few varieties that I have grown successfully:

Aunt Ruby's German Green is an heirloom variety with an indeterminate growing habit. I love to layer these with Brandywines, Golden Jubilee, and

White Wonders on a platter, and then sprinkle them with some diced red onion and chopped basil, chives and parsley. This makes a delicious and beautiful presentation. It is an 80-day variety.

Better Boy holds the Guinness record of producing 324 pounds of fruit from one plant. But I am sure that did not take place in the Rocky Mountain West. It is an indeterminate that sets deep red meaty fruit that can weigh nearly a pound each.

Black from Tula is a Russian heirloom that sets fruit in 80 to 85 days. The fruit is very dark chocolate colored. It is not a heavy producer, but the flavor is great, one of my favorites.

Brandywine is one of the best tasting heirlooms, but it is also a 90-day tomato. It sets large beefsteak type fruit on indeterminate vines. It is a heavy producer if you have a long season. Many consider this to be the best of all tomatoes.

Burpee Long Keeper is a determinate heirloom. It produces heavily. The nice thing about this tomato is that it will keep as long as 6 to 12 weeks. I have actually had ripe tomatoes to slice for Christmas dinner with this tomato.

Caspian Pink is the one some folks pick over Brandywine. This indeterminate 80 day tomato has light red flesh.

Cherokee Purple is an 80- to 90-day heirloom with large oblate fruit. It is an indeterminate and is very tolerant of most common tomato diseases. I really like the flavor of this one.

Cold Set is a determinate of 65 days. It is another open-pollinated variety. This is a tomato you can plant right in the ground instead of growing and transplanting. It has 3 to 4 inch fruit that is bright red.

Early Girl, an indeterminate hybrid, is an old standby in this area and comes in at an amazing 52 days. It sets bright red, firm 6 ounce fruits of great flavor.

Golden Jubilee is a 72-day indeterminate heirloom. It has mild flavor and low acidity and is a heavy producer.

Husky Red is a 68-day dwarf indeterminate. It is a hybrid that is perfect for container growing and produces over a long period. This also comes in Husky Gold.

Matina, an indeterminate, is an heirloom tomato and is listed as 58 days. It often bears tomatoes that weigh 4 ounces or more.

Mr. Stripey is a mild flavored indeterminate heirloom that sets low acid fruits with yellow flesh and pink centers. The fruits are the size of plums. It is an 80-day tomato.

Patio is a 70-day hybrid with a determinate habit. This is a great container plant and produces a good tasting fruit.

Stupice is another indeterminate heirloom. It is a 60-day variety that makes 2-3 inch fruits with really great flavor.

Subarctic Plenty is a determinate 51-day tomato that ripens extra early. This is an open-pollinated variety that has been around for a long time.

White Wonder is an indeterminate plant that takes 80 to 90 days to ripen. The fruit is white when ripe. It is sweet flavored and mild. It makes a nice contrast to red tomatoes sliced on a plate or in a salad.

Yellow Pear is a small variety, like a cherry tomato, but yellow and pear shaped. The plant is a very prolific producer of sweet yellow fruits. It is an indeterminate heirloom that produces in 78 days.

These are just a few of the many varieties that are available. After you have grown some different kinds of tomatoes, you will have your own favorites. Ask neighbors or gardening friends for suggestions, if you are not sure what you want to plant.

Remember when you read your seed package and it says 60 days or 72 days, for ripe tomatoes that means 60 or 72 days from transplanting, not 60 or 72 days from the time you plant your seeds. So if your goal is ripe tomatoes by the 4th of July, you must have the plants in the ground or in their pots by the first of May for a 60-day tomato and sooner than that for a longer growing one.

Cheryl Anderson Wright

In the Garden

Cheryl Anderson Wright

Where and When to Plant

I garden in raised beds. I use an intensive method of planting to make the best use of my space and because I hate weeding. Things grow better in dirt that is not compacted by my walking on it. I also use walls of water to extend my growing season. I can generally get my plants into the ground nearly a month before the last frost-free date, which gives me earlier tomatoes than my friends and neighbors.

If you have a regular garden area, you can still use the bed method. You simply pile the dirt into squares or rectangles, leaving walking space between them. Three

Cheryl Anderson Wright

feet is a good width, because you can reach across it to weed, plant and harvest. Make each bed as long as you like. Leave a couple of feet between the beds to walk on. By planting things thickly enough in soil rich in organic matter, you can avoid most weeding. You will still have a few weeds here and there, but they will be easy to pull out.

Or you can plant your garden using the conventional row method. Whatever way you choose to grow your tomatoes, remember that tomatoes are susceptible to even a light frost, so unless you use row covers or walls of water or some other type of protection you can not plant outside until after all danger of frost is past. That date for our area is around May 15th, but as I said before, most years we are still getting snow in June. You can check with your county extension agent to find out what the last frost date is for your area.

If you plant your tomatoes and have a late freeze or snow, cover them with old blankets or tarps or whatever you have on hand and you might save them.

Container Planting

You can garden perfectly well in containers, if you live in an apartment or if you have a lovely expanse of lawn that you don't want to disturb. Five gallon nursery buckets or paint buckets with drain holes drilled in the bottoms of them work well for containers, if you don't want to spend the money for commercially made pots. Make sure whatever you use has good drainage

I like to make my own mixture to fill these containers. Mix a twenty-pound bag of potting soil and a twenty-pound bag of composted manure together. Stir in a bag of vermiculite or perlite and mix well.

Fill the containers with this mixture. If you don't want the soil to come out the holes in the bottom of your container, you can lay a coffee filter over them. This will keep the soil in while still allowing the pot to drain. Once the pots are filled, add 1 cup of bone meal, 6 tablespoons of Epsom salts and 1/2 cup of kelp meal for each of the pots. Then I like to add about a cup of a 5-10-10 slow release organic fertilizer.

Mix all the ingredients well.

Water the containers and let the water drain. Then water them again. Once the pots have drained, they are ready to plant.

Make a small hole in the center of the pot.

Carefully take your seedling from the growing cell and put it into the hole right up to the first set of leaves. This will result in a much stronger plant, as the tomato will root all along the stem that is placed underground. Firm the soil around the plants and water lightly.

Now place the plants where they will get as much sun as possible, at least 10 to 12 hours a day. This may involve carrying your plants out on warm days and back in on cools nights, but when you enjoy that first vine-ripened tomato on the 4th of July you will know your efforts have been rewarded.

Walls of Water

Walls of water are a godsend to gardeners in our area. They keep your tomatoes warm at night and allow you to plant earlier than would otherwise be possible. I like to set up my walls about the first of May. I leave them for a week to warm the water they contain and the soil. Then I move them to the side, prepare my holes and plant my tomatoes, and then I move the walls back over the tomatoes and close the tops. This makes a mini greenhouse with the precise environment tomatoes love.

As the weather warms and the plants grow, I open the walls and put my tomato cages inside. I leave my walls on all summer. Some people take them off. This is your choice. Leaving them on works well for me, especially when we get that last snow of the year.

Staking

Most tomatoes, especially the indeterminate varieties, will need to be staked. You can build your own stakes by using one inch in diameter tree trimmings about seven or eight feet long. Make a teepee of three sticks and tie them together at the top with twine. You can then tie shorter pieces of wood between the sides to make a stable support and place it over your tomato.

You can buy square tomato cages, or round ones. There are tomato spirals available. To use these you simply place the spiral into the ground by the tomato and then guide it through the spirals as the plant grows. You can use a bamboo pole and tie the plant to it with pieces of old nylon or plastic coated wire.

You can make cages out of pieces of woven wire. Eight feet of woven wire makes a cage that is 2 1/2 to 3 feet in diameter. Cut the wire, and then bend it into a circle. Bend the cut edges of one end over the loops of the rectangles on the other end to make your circle. Place this over your tomato plant for support.

Fertilizers

I am a proponent of organic fertilizers, but to each his own. There are certainly many fertilizers out there such as Miracle Gro for tomatoes. I prepare the holes in my garden the same way I prepare the soil for my container plants. I add bonemeal, Epsom salts, and a slow release fertilizer that is 5-10-10. Or else I add Tomatoes Alive, an organic fertilizer from Gardens Alive. Weak compost tea or fish emulsions are two more good choices. Whatever I add, I make sure it's organic, but that's a choice each gardener must make.

Mulch

Once the tomatoes are up and growing, I add a layer of compost about two inches thick around each plant. I try to renew the compost around the first part of July and again in August because it is feeding the soil as well as the plants. You can also use plastic mulch if you like. This will keep in the moisture and warm the soil.

Mulching, especially with organic mulches, provides many benefits as long as it is done properly. It maintains soil moisture, helps control weeds, insulates the soil from both heat and cold, improves the soil structure and fertility, and keeps fruits and vegetables off the ground. You may choose to mulch your garden, especially if you live where watering is restricted.

There are many different organic types of mulch you can use:

- shredded leaves
- compost
- grass clippings
- newspaper
- pine needles
- straw
- wood chips
- shredded bark

These types of mulches will add organic matter to your garden and improve your soil.

Once again, make sure anything you are using is pesticide and herbicide free. I know a gardener who carefully mulched his entire garden with grass clippings he got free from the cemetery. What he didn't know was, they had spread a weed and feed product on the grass the week before they mowed. The grass not only killed his garden, it killed the ground for several years.

And as beneficial as mulch is, it can be overdone. Two to four inches is generally enough. Do not pile mulch around the stem of a plant or the trunk of a tree or bush as this can cause many problems you don't want to deal with. Make sure the area you are mulching has good drainage.

You can also use plastic mulch, which comes in black, clear and red. Red is said to enhance the growth of tomatoes. There is also a material called ground cloth that suppresses weeds but allows air and moisture through. These materials will either have to be pinned down to the ground or have something like bark or stones put on them to hold them down.

There is a new material that I have just discovered called garden bio-film. It is made from corn and is 100% biodegradable and compostable. You can purchase this product at:

www.biogroupusa.com

Cheryl Anderson Wright

It is guaranteed to degrade after about ninety days, although in our climate, I wouldn't be surprised if it took at least six months.

There is also red plastic mulch that is said to raise the production of tomatoes by twenty percent. I may have to try that one!

Harvesting & Saving Seed

Cheryl Anderson Wright

Harvest your tomatoes as soon as they are ripe. You can either eat them fresh or preserve them for winter. If the frost hits before all your tomatoes are ripe, harvest the green ones, and spread them out in a single layer in boxes or on a table. Let them lay until they are ripe and then preserve them in whatever manner you choose. Or you can fry them or make them into green tomato pickles.

Once you have harvested all your tomatoes, clean up your garden plots. Pull all the tomato cages and stack them away for the winter. Empty the walls of water and stand them upside down to drain. Then put them in a box or a five gallon bucket to store for the winter. Clean off all the garden debris. If you have had any problems with diseases or pests, take all the refuse to the garbage. If you have been problem-free, then put everything in your compost pile.

Your garden is now ready to plant a winter cover crop for green manure, if you so choose. Green manuring is another good way to enrich your soil. There are many good articles on the subject. Winter rye is a good cover crop. You can buy the seed from many of the sources listed in the back of this book. I think I will try it myself this fall.

If you have grown either heirloom tomatoes or open pollinated varieties, you may also want to save your own seed. The seed needs to be fermented before saving, so this is how you go about it: Cut the bottom end off the tomatoes, and then squeeze them into a clean jar. Most of the seeds will come out with the pulp and juice and fall into the jar.

Put only one variety of tomato in a jar and label it so you will know exactly what you have.

Let the jar sit in a warm place, at about seventy-two degrees. The seeds should ferment and become moldy in about two days and the good seeds will fall to the bottom. Carefully pour off the liquid and mold.

Pour the seeds and the last of the liquid into a sieve, adding water if necessary to get them all out of the jar. Rinse with cool running water. Rub and rinse until all the residue is gone from the seeds. Then dump them onto clean paper towels or newspapers and let them lay in a warm place until dry. Store in clean jars in a cool dark place. Be sure to label the jar with the variety of seed.

Cheryl Anderson Wright

Recipes

Cheryl Anderson Wright

Once you get your tomatoes growing, your harvest is in full swing, and you have eaten your fill of plain, fresh, flavorful homegrown tomatoes, you will probably want to branch out and try them other ways. Here are some of my favorite recipes and I know you will either have or be able to find ones of your own, too.

Also you might want to try canning, freezing or drying them if you have a real surplus and would like to save some for winter use. If you find that you want to do a lot of preserving, I would suggest that you buy a copy of *Putting Food By*. This is an excellent reference book written by Janet C. Greene. *Stocking Up* by Carol Hupping is another good book on preserving your harvest.

Cheryl Anderson Wright

Soups

Cheryl Anderson Wright

Tomato Soup

This soup is much like Campbell's without all the salt, sugar and preservatives, and with much more flavor. If you have a pressure canner, you can make this soup in larger quantities and can it.

4 pounds or 8 cups of diced ripe tomatoes

1 or 2 medium sized onions, peeled and diced

1 sweet pepper seeded and diced

1/2 stalk celery

1/4 cup diced carrot

1 tsp. minced garlic

Cook all together until the onion is transluscent and carrots are soft. Then run the mixture through a sieve or food mill. Put the resulting juice back on to cook. Mix together:

2 Tbs. of sugar (optional)

1 1/2 Tbs. lemon juice or vinegar

1 or 2 tsp. salt, or to taste

4 Tbs. cornstarch

Mix these ingredients together. Add enough water to make it a nice smooth consistency if necessary.

Pour this slowly into the tomato juice, stirring as you pour, and cook until slightly thickened. Stir in a couple of Tbs. of minced fresh parsley and a Tbs. of minced chives. Dip into a serving bowl and drizzle the hot soup with a little plain yogurt or sour cream and a small sprinkle of minced parsley or chives for garnish. Serve hot.

You can double this recipe and pour it into hot sterilized jars and pressure can it at 10 pounds of pressure for 20 minutes, or you can make up the first part of the recipe and freeze it, then add the sugar, salt, lemon juice, cornstarch and herbs when you get hungry for a bowl of homemade soup on some cold winter day.

Fresh Herbed Tomato Soup

1/2 cup diced onion

1/4 cup diced celery

1/4 cup diced carrots

2 cloves garlic, minced

2 Tbs. butter

1 bay leaf

1/4 cup minced fresh parsley
or 2 Tbs. dried

1/2 tsp. dried thyme

1/2 tsp. dried marjoram

2 tsp. dried basil

2 cups chicken stock

4 large tomatoes peeled and diced
or 2 pints canned tomatoes

Brown onion, carrots, celery, and garlic in butter until soft. Add herbs and tomatoes. Cook about 10 minutes. Stir in stock and simmer for 15 to 20 minutes. You can add a cup or so of cooked brown rice or cooked pasta for a hardier soup if you wish.

Gazpacho

This is cold tomato soup. It is my favorite dish for lunch on a hot summer afternoon. If it is too early in the season for fresh tomatoes, hopefully you still have some frozen or canned from last summer. To freeze extra tomatoes, wash them and remove the stems. Put them into a freezer bag and put them in the freezer. When you are ready to make your gazpacho or spaghetti sauce or whatever, run them under hot water to remove the peels then dice them up or put them in the blender and chop them.

3 large tomatoes, peeled and cored
or 4 cups of canned or frozen tomatoes

1 sweet pepper, seeded and diced
(any color, but yellow or green
is pretty with the red of the tomatoes)

1/2 of a small sweet onion, like Vidalia or Walla Walla
or 2 to 4 shallots or scallions, peeled and diced

1/2 stalk of celery, diced

2 cloves of garlic, minced

salt and pepper to taste

2 to 3 cups of chicken or vegetable broth,
or tomato juice
or a combination of the two

a dash of Tabasco or other hot sauce
1 diced avocado or cucumber
may be added or used as a garnish
2 tsp. of lime or lemon juice
1 Tbs. minced parsley
1 Tbs. minced chives
1 tsp. minced basil

Mix all the ingredients together and let the mixture sit in the refrigerator until cold, unless you are using frozen tomatoes, in which case you may have to let it sit on the counter to finish thawing. But do serve the soup cold. Good hardy bread with some red pepper cream cheese or tapenade goes really well with this soup and makes it a full meal.

Cheryl Anderson Wright

Chesapeake Bay Crab Soup

2 Tbs. olive oil

1 carrot, diced

1 medium onion, diced

3 cups of chicken broth

3 cups of beef broth

3 – 4 cups of peeled, diced potatoes

3 – 4 cups diced tomatoes

1 tsp. fish seasoning
(the recipe for this is in High Country Herbs)

1 pound of crabmeat, clams, shrimp or scallops
or a combination of all of them
(even add a little lobster if you happen to
have some left over!)

2 Tbs. chopped parsley

Sauté the carrot, onion and potatoes in oil until lightly browned. Add broth, tomatoes and seasonings. Simmer covered until vegetables are tender. Add crab or clams or shrimp or scallops or a combination. Heat through. Serve at once with a nice crusty bread for dipping. This is a great soup for one of those blustery winter days. It makes you feel all warm and toasty inside and out.

Cheryl Anderson Wright

Salads

Cheryl Anderson Wright

Italian Bread Salad

To make this salad, use a good hearty Italian or French bread. The Italian bread I have given you the recipe for will work well. Cut about 2 cups of bread into cubes and let it dry overnight. Then, when you are ready to make the salad, soak the bread cubes in water for about 1 minute, then drain and squeeze out any excess water. Put the bread cubes in a bowl.

Add:

3 large tasty tomatoes, diced

2 sweet onions, peeled and diced
or use shallots or scallions instead

1/4 cup parsley, chopped

3 Tbs. capers

1/4 cups fresh basil, chopped

Dressing:

3 Tbs. olive oil or more to taste

2 cloves of garlic, minced

2 Tbs. balsamic vinegar

1 tsp. sugar (optional)

salt and pepper to taste

Cheryl Anderson Wright

Mix all these ingredients together and pour over the salad. Toss well. Allow to sit at room temperature, covered, for flavors to blend.

Tomato Mozzarella Salad

Slice several ripe tomatoes, about 6 or so

1/4 pound mozzarella, thinly sliced

Layer these two alternately on a platter

Dressing:

3 Tbs. olive oil

3 Tbs. fresh lemon juice

1 clove garlic minced

1/2 of a small red onion, diced

2 Tbs. fresh basil leaves, chopped

Mix together in a blender. Blend only until the onion is finely chopped. Allow to sit for about half an hour for flavors to blend then pour over the layered tomatoes and mozzarella. Sprinkle with toasted pine nuts or sunflower seeds, if desired.

Tomato and Onion Salad

Layer alternate slices of red onion and tomatoes on a platter. You can also add slices of mozzarella, if you like. Instead of sprinkling it with pine nuts, you can sprinkle it with a mixture of chopped herbs, about 2 Tbs. of mixed parsley, chives and basil. Some Greek olives or peperoncinos along the edges make a nice garnish. Then drizzle this dressing over everything and serve.

Dressing:
1/4 cup olive oil
1 clove garlic, minced
1/2 tsp. dried parsley or 1 1/2 tsp. fresh parsley, minced
1/2 tsp. dried Mexican oregano
or 1 1/2 tsp. fresh, minced
(if you can't find Mexican oregano, you can substitute basil, but **not** regular oregano, which is too strong)
1 Tbs. lime juice
1 Tbs. Worcestershire sauce
1 Tbs. soy sauce

Stir together until well blended and drizzle over the salad. Of course, if you would rather you can dice the tomatoes, onions and Mozzarella, put everything in a bowl and drizzle the dressing over that. Dip up the dressing with some Italian or French bread. Delicious.

Tomato Macaroni Salad

This is a summer standard at our house because my husband loves it.

1 cup of macaroni,
cooked until it reaches the desired doneness

1/2 green, red, or yellow sweet pepper, seeded and diced

5 or 6 green onions (scallions), peeled and sliced
(be sure to include a portion of the green part of the onion)
or use 1/4 cup diced onions or shallots

1/2 cup sliced black olives (optional)

1 – 2 large ripe tomato, diced

1 Tbs. parsley, minced

1 Tbs. chives, minced

2 Tbs. Italian bottled salad dressing

Enough mayonnaise or Miracle Whip to moisten

Mix all together, cover and place in the refrigerator to chill and allow the flavors to blend. This is a quick easy salad to go with grilled chicken or fish. It will also stand alone for lunch.

Cheryl Anderson Wright

Breads

Cheryl Anderson Wright

Italian Bread

Good homemade soup deserves a good homemade bread to go with it. And with the advent of bread machines, making bread is easy enough for anyone to do.

1 Tbs. olive oil

1/2 cup plus 2 Tbs. water

1/2 cup milk

1 tsp. salt

2 3/4 cups unbleached white flour,
or use 1/2 whole wheat and 1/2 unbleached white flour

1 1/2 tsp. sugar

1 1/2 tsp. bread machine yeast

Place all ingredients into the bread machine in the order given, turn the machine to the dough cycle and let it do its thing. When it is finished, take the dough out and form it into a long loaf, or a round loaf if you would rather, and let it rise on a greased baking sheet that has been dusted with cornmeal. Let it rise for 30 minutes to an hour or until doubled in size. Then bake at 375° for 30 minutes or until the loaf is golden brown and sounds hollow when tapped. You can also add 1 Tbs. onion flakes and 1 tsp. Italian seasoning (recipe in *High Country Herbs*) to make an onion herb bread that makes delicious grilled cheese sandwiches. Or you can let the bread bake in your bread machine.

Cheryl Anderson Wright

Tomato Basil Bread

This bread goes well with soup or salad. It is a delicious spread with a little cream cheese or any one of the spreads from *High Country Herbs.*

1 cup water

1/4 cup slow roast tomatoes or dried tomatoes, soaked in boiling water, drained and diced

2 cloves of garlic crushed or 1 tsp. minced garlic

4 cups of unbleached white flour, or use 1/2 white and 1/2 whole wheat

1/2 cup Asiago, Parmesan or Romano cheese, grated

2 Tbs. sugar

2 tsp. salt

1 1/2 Tbs. chopped fresh basil leaves or 2 tsp. dried basil

1 Tbs. chopped fresh parsley or 1 1/2 tsp. dried parsley

1 3/4 tsp. bread machine yeast

Place all ingredients into the bread machine in the order given, turn the machine to the dough cycle and let it do its thing. When it is finished, take the dough out and form it into a long loaf or a round loaf, if you would rather, on a greased baking sheet that has been dusted with cornmeal. Let it rise for 30 minutes to an hour or until doubled in size. Then bake at 350° for 30 minutes or until the loaf is golden brown and sounds hollow when tapped. You can also let the bread bake in your bread machine.

Cheryl Anderson Wright

Appetizers

Cheryl Anderson Wright

Tomatoes Stuffed with Goat Cheese and Chives
Serves 6 to 8

9 large Roma tomatoes

1/2 lb. mild, creamy goat cheese (chevre)

heaping cup chopped fresh chives

1/4 cup olive oil
or enough to make the cheese mixture creamy

fresh ground pepper to taste

Cut tomatoes in half lengthwise and scoop out all the seeds. Place them cut side down on paper towels and drain for at least 30 minutes. Place cheese, chives, oil and a generous grinding of pepper into a bowl and mix until well blended, smooth and creamy. Divide the cheese mixture evenly among the tomato halves. Garnish with chopped parsley or chives or pine nuts. Serve at room temperature.

If you don't care for goat cheese, then make this with cream cheese. Use yogurt to thin instead of olive oil and a little milk if needed. You can also stir in some diced dried tomatoes, or some pepper pesto (from *High Country Herbs*) or chopped pine nuts or sunflower seeds.

Salsa

1-15 oz can diced tomatoes
or 3 fresh tomatoes peeled and diced

1 small onion diced or 2 Tbs. dried minced onion
or 6 scallions or 2 – 3 shallots, diced

1 can diced green chilies
or 1 Anaheim pepper, seeded and diced

1 sweet pepper, diced (optional)

1 avocado, peeled and diced (optional)

1 cucumber, peeled, seeded, and diced (optional)

1 Tbs. chopped parsley or cilantro

1 clove garlic, minced

1/4 tsp. cumin

1 Tbs. lime juice (fresh is best)

1/2 tsp. oregano or basil (optional)

Mix all together, let sit for about an hour to let the flavors
blend, and serve with any Mexican food.

Slow Roasted Tomatoes

Preheat oven to 250°. Lightly oil a cookie sheet.

Wash Roma tomatoes and slice in half lengthwise. Place on baking sheet. Lightly spray with olive oil and sprinkle with salt, pepper and a mixture of herbs, like parsley, chives and basil, which have been finely chopped. Bake them for about an hour, stirring them now and then so they won't burn. Add more olive oil if they seem too dry.

When they are almost dry (about 4 hours) remove them from the oven and let them cool. Store them in a jar in the refrigerator or freeze.

These are great on sandwiches, or just with bread and cheese. You can use them on pizza with artichokes and a little mozzarella and a few black olives. You can dice them up and mix them with cream cheese and some chives, and maybe a few toasted pine nuts, chopped. Or chop them and mix them with sour cream or plain yogurt with some herbs for either a spread or thin it with a little milk and make a salad dressing. You can use them in tomato bread. I am sure you can come up with some more uses for these too.

Tomato Basil Salsa

6 – 8 tomatoes, seeds removed and diced
2 scallions thinly sliced
3 Tbs. olive oil
3 Tbs. balsamic vinegar
1 tsp. minced garlic
1/2 tsp. lemon juice
1/4 cup sliced black olives (optional)
4 Tbs. minced fresh basil

Mix all together and serve on pasta. Or toast slices of French bread, rub with a clove of garlic and top with this mixture. Add a sprinkle of Parmesan cheese or toasted pine nuts if you want.

Cheryl Anderson Wright

Main Dishes & Sauces

Cheryl Anderson Wright

White Pizza

This is a great pizza recipe. This crust is one of the best I have ever eaten. Linda Ermer generously offered to share her recipe with us. It is much better than any pizza you can buy, so try it. This pizza could get you addicted to the homemade variety.

Crust:

Be sure all your ingredients are at room temperature.

Makes one crust.

6-7 ounces of water

3/4 tsp. salt

2 Tbs. olive oil

3 tsp. sugar

2 1/2 cups unbleached flour

1 3/4 tsp. active dry yeast

Place the ingredients into bread machine in order listed. Use the "dough only" setting on the bread machine. The kneading and rising usually takes about 1 1/2 hours. Let the dough rest for about 10 minutes after the machine finishes its cycles.

Preheat the oven to 400°. Lightly oil a pizza pan with olive oil and sprinkle it with cornmeal. Spread or roll the crust on alightly floured surface until it is the size of the pizza pan. Carefully lift the crust and place it in the prepared pan. Brush the crust lightly with olive oil and crushed garlic.

Cheryl Anderson Wright

Topping:

1 large tomato, thinly sliced

6 – 8 thin slices of mozzarella

1 medium sweet onion, thinly sliced

1 red, orange, or yellow pepper,

seeded and sliced into rings

1 1/2 cups fresh mushrooms, sliced

Cook the onions, mushrooms and peppers in the microwave for approximately 2 minutes on high to soften them. Cover the crust with the slices of tomato, then the cheese, then the rest of the vegetables. You may also add sliced black or green olives, canned artichokes or any other ingredients you like. You can put basil pesto on the crust, or spread it lightly with Ranch dressing or Parmesan cheese for a different taste. You can use half whole wheat flour in the crust, if you prefer. Or use a different kind of cheese. Feta cheese might be to your taste, or a sprinkling of chopped herbs. (You *know* I think everything is better with herbs.)

My grandson likes to add pepperoni, ham, Canadian bacon, and/or sausage to his pizza then top it all with cheese. Just experiment with toppings until you find what you really like, then go for it!

Bake at 400° fo 20-30 minutes until the crust is crisp and golden.

Ruth Fiori's Spaghetti Sauce

Ruth was my neighbor when I was first married. She was and is a gracious lady and a great cook. She took me under her wing and taught me many things, but one of the best was how to make this spaghetti sauce. It makes wonderful spaghetti, lasagna, chicken cacciatore, pizza, or just about anything else. It is also a good sauce for dipping your bread.

2 lb. beef neck or rib bones

1 lb. chicken wings or backs

1 large onion, diced

2-3 cloves garlic, minced

2 Tbs. parsley

2 bay leaves

1 - 2 Tbs. Italian seasoning

1 can tomato paste and 4 large cans tomato sauce

or 16 cups of peeled crushed tomatoes

1/2 cup good red or white wine

1 tsp. sugar (optional)

Salt and pepper to taste

Brown beef and chicken in 350° oven for 1 to 2 hours. Remove from oven and cover with water. Simmer for 1 to 2 hours until meat is tender. Remove meat and bones from broth and add all the rest of the ingredients to the broth. Simmer until thick, 6 to 8 hours. Remove meat from bones and either put it back into the cooked sauce or save for another use. You can prepare the broth the day before and refrigerate it and then remove the fat if desired. This makes a large amount so you can freeze leftover sauce to use at a later date.

Fresh Tomato Sauce

1/4 cup olive oil

4 cloves garlic minced

1 medium onion, finely chopped

16 cups of peeled, diced very ripe tomatoes

1/4 cup chopped parsley

1 1/2 cups chicken, beef or vegetable stock

1 tsp. dried marjoram
or 1 Tbs. fresh marjoram, chopped

1 tsp. dried rosemary
or 1 Tbs. fresh rosemary, chopped

1/2 cup good white or red wine

Heat olive oil in a heavy kettle and stir in the onions and garlic. Cook and stir until the onions are limp. Add the rest of the ingredients and bring to a boil. Lower the heat and simmer about 4 hours or until the sauce is thick.

Leftover sauce freezes well.

Baked Tomatoes with Peppers and Herbs

I love this dish. Often I will add a small eggplant and/or a chopped onion to the mix. This with a good hardy bread and some tapenade is a whole meal for me. Most folks will want to add a grilled salmon steak or a chicken breast though.

4 - 6 large bell peppers (red or yellow)

Roast peppers until the skin is blackened, then place in a bowl and cover the bowl with a plate. Let the peppers steam until cool enough to handle, then remove the peelings, seed them, and cut them into strips. While the peppers are cooling take about 6 tomatoes (a combination of red and yellow is good), dip them in boiling water until the skins loosen. Peel them, gently squeeze out the seeds if desire and cut into large chunks.

Mix together:

1 tsp. minced garlic
2 Tbs. chopped fresh parsley
2 Tbs. capers
1 Tbs. fresh marjoram or basil, chopped

3 Tbs. olive oil
Salt and pepper to taste

Place peppers and tomatoes in a large oven proof pie pan. Cover with foil and bake at 400° for about 20 minutes.

Cool slightly and serve.

You can add diced eggplant, zucchini and onions to this mix and have an oven baked ratatouille.

Dried Tomato Pesto
Makes enough for 6 servings of pasta

20 oven-dried tomato halves

1/8 cup toasted pine nuts

1/4 cup Parmesan cheese

3/4 cup olive oil

1/2 cup packed basil leaves

In a food processor, combine tomato halves, pine nuts, cheese and basil. Slowly add the olive oil. Blend until smooth. This is very good as a sauce for pizza, to spread on bread, or as a sauce for pasta.

Grilled Chicken Breast
with Tomato Cream Sauce

6 chicken breasts

salt and pepper to taste

1 Tbs. olive oil

Heat the olive oil in a heavy skillet. Salt and pepper the chicken breasts and cook them in the olive oil until they are lightly browned. Turn and brown the other side. Cook until the breasts are done, but still moist.

Sauce:

1 1/2 cups fresh tomato sauce
or the same of canned sauce

1/3 cup Half and Half

1/2 tsp. dried marjoram
or 1 1/2 tsp. fresh marjoram, chopped

Mix together. Put 1/2 cup of the mixture in the bottom of a greased glass 9 x 13 baking dish. Lay the chicken breasts on top and cover with the rest of the sauce. Cut up a jar of artichokes and put around the edges.

Mix 1/4 cup of grated Parmesan with 1 cup of grated mozzarella. Sprinkle over the top of the sauce. Bake at 325 ° for 25 to 30 minutes or until cheese melts and the dish is nicely browned.

Cheryl Anderson Wright

Side Dishes

Cheryl Anderson Wright

Fried Green Tomatoes
Makes 4 servings

3 or 4 large green tomatoes
sliced into 1/4 inch thick slices

Sprinkle slices lightly with Worcestershire sauce and a dash of hot pepper sauce.

1/4 cup fine cornmeal with 1/2cup flour mixed together

In a heavy skillet, put enough cooking oil to cover the bottom to about 1/4 inch.

Dip tomato slices in flour mixture. Shake off excess. Fry in oil until golden brown, turn and brown the other side. Do not crowd the skillet. Drain on paper towels. Serve at once.

You can also fry solid ripe tomatoes this way.

Cheryl Anderson Wright

Green Tomato Pickles

In the South there are restaurants that serve all the catfish and hush puppies you can eat. Many times this pickle is also served. I hunted for many years for a recipe to make these pickles and finally came up with this one. This recipe makes 5 to 6 pints of tomato pickles.

2 quarts of green tomatoes, quartered
or cut into bite size pieces
3 Tbs. canning salt

Choose firm green tomatoes. The end of the gardening season is a good time to make these pickles. Sprinkle the cut up tomatoes with salt and let them sit overnight.

The next morning drain the tomatoes well. Ready 6 pint canning jars, washing and scalding them with boiling water.

Mix together:
2 cups of cider vinegar
1 cup dark brown sugar
1 cup sugar
3 Tbs. mustard seed
1/2 tsp. celery seed
1 1/2 tsp. tumeric

Stir everything together in a large kettle and bring it to a boil. Then add 4 cups of sliced onions, bring to a boil and boil another 5 minutes. Stir in the drained tomatoes, bring back to a boil and boil for 5 more minutes.

Loosely pack the tomatoes and onions into the canning jars. Cover with the syrup. Run a knife down into the jars to remove any air bubbles. Fill with syrup to 1/2 inch below the top of the jar. Wipe the rim of the jar and put lid and ring on the jar. Tighten the lid. Process in a boiling water bath for 10 minutes.

Cheryl Anderson Wright

Resource Guide

There are many sources for tomato seeds and plants including your local nursery and the many seed catalogues you probably get in the mail. Here are some of my favorites.

Totally Tomatoes

334 West Stroud Street, Randolph, WI 53956,

Toll free phone (800) 345–5977,

Website: www.totallytomato.com. They have every tomato seed you can imagine, plus peppers and a few other vegetables. They also have a selection of supplies for growing tomatoes, such as mulch and fertilizers.

Seeds of Change

PO Box 15700, Santa Fe, NM 87592-1500

Toll-free phone (888) 762-7333,

Website: www.seedsofchange.com. They have a wide selection of 100 % organic seeds and supplies, including many unusual and rare varieties.

Planet Natural

1612 Gold Avenue, Bozeman, MT 59715

Toll-free phone (800) 289-6656

Website: www.planetnatural.com. They have a great variety of natural products for your home, lawn and garden. Online they have an even larger selection with many heirloom seed offerings.

The Cook's Garden

PO Box 535, Londonderry, VT 05148

Toll-free phone (800) 457-9703

Website: www.cooksgarden.com. A very diverse collection of seeds, garden supplies, kitchen supplies, books, prints and calendars is presented in this catalogue, including some unusual and hard to find varieties.

Gardens Alive

5100 Schenley Place, Lawrenceburg, IN 47025

Phone: 513 354 -1484

Website: www.GardensAlive.com. This catalogue offers many different kinds of fertilizers and pest controls as well as a great deal of useful information on pests and plant diseases and the damage they cause.

Gardener's Supply Company

128 Intervale Road, Burlington, VT 05401

Toll–free phone (800) 427-3363

Website: www.gardeners.com. Here you'll find anything you can think of and many things you never dreamed of in the way of gardening supplies. A wonderful wishbook for any gardener.

Territorial Seed Company

PO Box 158, Cottage Grove, OR 97424-0061

Phone 541 942-9547

Website: www.territorialseed.com. This is the place to buy plants as well as seeds and many varieties of herbs, as well as all kinds of garden and kitchen supplies.

J.W. Jung Seed Company

335 S. High Street, Randolph, WI 53957-0001

Toll-free phone (800) 247-5864

Website: www.jungseed.com. Jung presents a great selection of garden seeds and plants.

Henry Fields

PO Box 397, Aurora, IN 47001-0397

Phone 513 354-1494. Website: www.HenryFields.com This is an old standby company with a large variety of reliable seeds and plants.

Cheryl Anderson Wright

Index

Cheryl Anderson Wright

CPSIA information can be obtained
at www.ICGtesting.com
Printed in the USA
LVHW04s2246101018
593104LV00001B/55/P

9 781932 636079